WAR & CONFLICT

BY
KIRSTY HOLMES

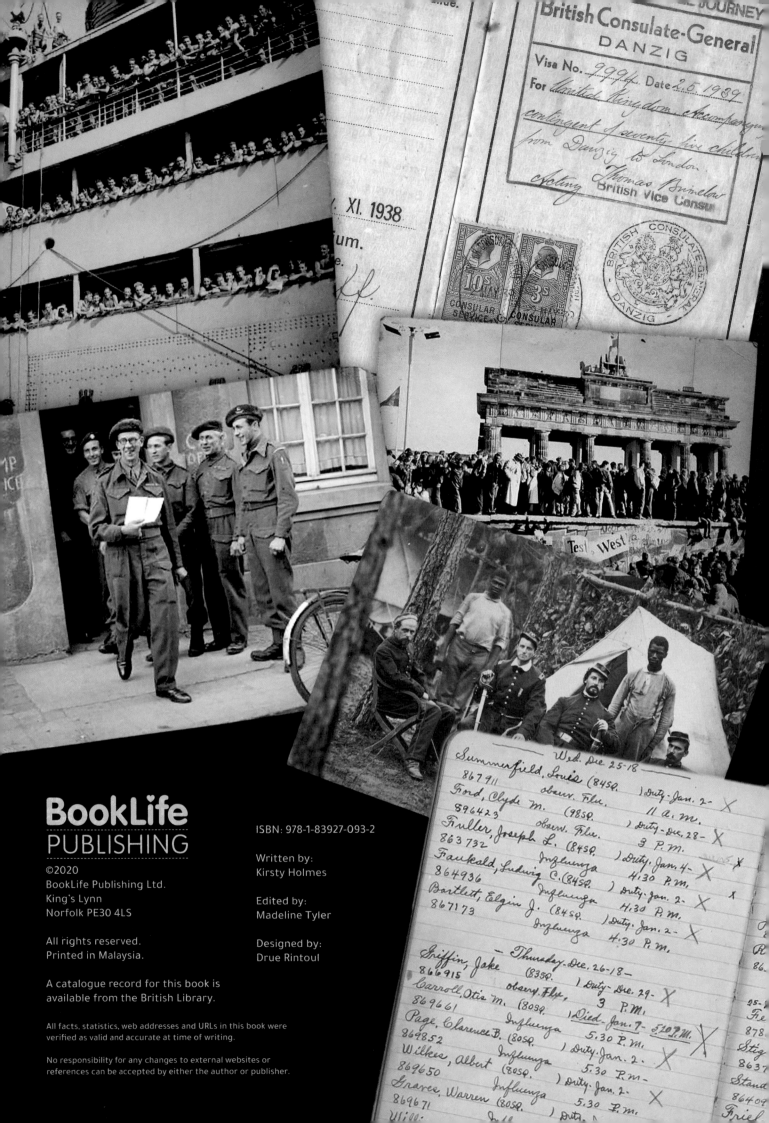

BookLife
PUBLISHING

©2020
BookLife Publishing Ltd.
King's Lynn
Norfolk PE30 4LS

All rights reserved.
Printed in Malaysia.

A catalogue record for this book is
available from the British Library.

All facts, statistics, web addresses and URLs in this book were
verified as valid and accurate at time of writing.

No responsibility for any changes to external websites or
references can be accepted by either the author or publisher.

ISBN: 978-1-83927-093-2

Written by:
Kirsty Holmes

Edited by:
Madeline Tyler

Designed by:
Drue Rintoul

CONTENTS

WORDS THAT LOOK LIKE <u>THIS</u> ARE EXPLAINED IN THE GLOSSARY ON PAGE 31.

THE MOVEMENT OF PEOPLE

That hink about the world. How many countries can you name? How many of those have you visited? There are hundreds of different countries in the world today, and many more have come and gone throughout history. As humans have built cities, countries and <u>empires</u>, we have pushed and pulled at the borders of our world, through war, conflict and invasion. For thousands of years, wars have shaped the movement of people.

Although we have not seen a world war in many years, smaller conflicts happen all the time and sometimes these become wars that can rage for many years. Fighting in and between countries leads to the movement of people, as troops are <u>deployed</u>, and countries are invaded and occupied. When a war is over, new borders are drawn. While some countries are erased, others are created and added to the world map. How does this affect the decisions that people make about their lives?

WHY MOVE?

People caught up in a war zone might leave for many reasons. If your country is at war, and the war is near where you live, it might not be safe to stay. If the war is not happening right where you live, other problems might make it difficult or impossible to stay in your country. Countries at war might not have much food, or have problems with <u>infrastructure</u>. Sometimes, people have no choice but to leave, and hope there will be a country left for them to return to one day.

WHAT'S WHAT?

Migration means movement. There are many different reasons for why a person might migrate, but this book will be focusing on war and conflict. Here are some words that you may come across.

CONFLICT: a strong disagreement, battle or struggle

ARMED CONFLICT: a conflict which is fought in physical battles using weapons

INTERNAL CONFLICT: when a war is being fought between two or more sides within the same country

WAR: a conflict between countries, areas or groups, which is usually fought in armed battles

CIVIL WAR: a war between different groups in the same country

WORLD WAR: a war that involves all or most of the major countries of the world

COLD WAR: when two countries are in conflict, but they fight using <u>spies</u> and <u>politics</u> rather than weapons or violence

INVASION: when one country enters another as its enemy; usually with an army

OCCUPATION: when an invading country remains in the country it has invaded and takes over

WAR AND CONFLICT

Countries that are very different in their culture, history and politics often have to live side by side, and sometimes it becomes no longer possible for these countries to agree. Countries and different groups of people usually try to fix issues by talking about them and trying to reach a <u>compromise</u>. This is called diplomacy.

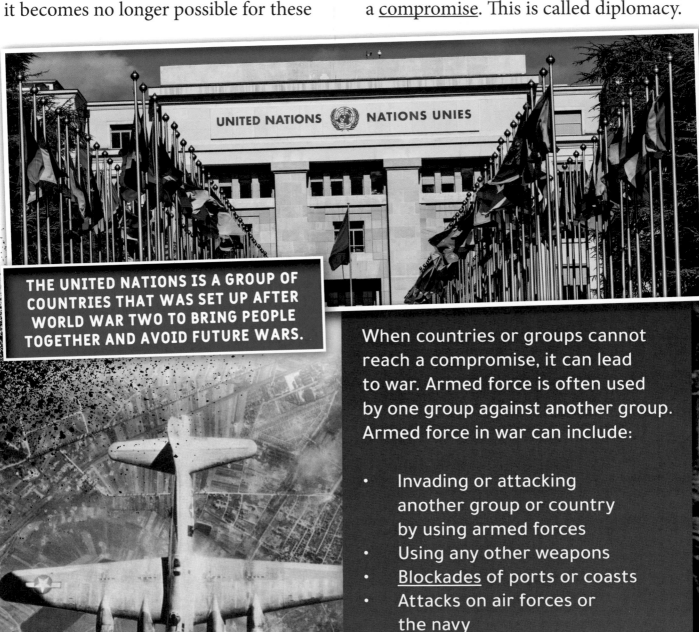

UNITED NATIONS 🌐 NATIONS UNIES

THE UNITED NATIONS IS A GROUP OF COUNTRIES THAT WAS SET UP AFTER WORLD WAR TWO TO BRING PEOPLE TOGETHER AND AVOID FUTURE WARS.

When countries or groups cannot reach a compromise, it can lead to war. Armed force is often used by one group against another group. Armed force in war can include:

- Invading or attacking another group or country by using armed forces
- Using any other weapons
- <u>Blockades</u> of ports or coasts
- Attacks on air forces or the navy

AN AMERICAN B-17 BOMBER FLYING OVER GERMANY, 1944

The aggressor is the country or group that starts the war. Aggressors may attack towns and cities by sending troops or launching missiles. They may stop food and other goods from reaching the country by blocking its ports or attacking the ships and planes that bring the food and goods in. As well as this, they may also stop the movement of people in and out of the country or area.

Wars can be short, or they can last for years. They need at least two sides but can include more.

LONG-RANGE MISSILES CAN BE LAUNCHED FROM OTHER COUNTRIES, OR OUT AT SEA.

THIS PHOTO SHOWS ADOLF HITLER, THE LEADER OF GERMANY AT THE TIME, WATCHING GERMAN TROOPS INVADE POLAND. AFTER THE INVASION STARTED, GREAT BRITAIN AND FRANCE DECLARED WAR ON GERMANY AND WORLD WAR TWO BEGAN.

BOOTS ON THE GROUND

When war breaks out, the first people on the move tend to be the troops. Soldiers might need to move within their own country in order to fight a civil war, or to defend their country from invading troops.

OFFICERS AND THEIR SERVANTS IN A CAMP IN 1864 DURING THE AMERICAN CIVIL WAR

OVER 60 MILLION TROOPS FOUGHT IN WORLD WAR ONE, AND MANY OF THESE WERE MOVED AROUND THE WORLD DURING THE FOUR YEARS OF THE WAR.

Soldiers might also need to move into another country to fight, or to protect an allied country from attack. Depending on the size of the war, many thousands or even millions of troops might move around the world.

During war, many soldiers live in camps. If the soldiers will be in the same place for a long time, they might stay in more long-lasting bases. Anywhere an army goes, it will also need to take the things that support it, too, such as equipment, food, medical supplies, animals, transport and weapons, as well as doctors, nurses and chefs. All of these people need somewhere to sleep, things to eat and a place to store all of their things. That is a lot of people and a lot of things.

BASES, LIKE THIS ONE IN BASRA, IRAQ, ARE HEAVILY PROTECTED.

AN ARMY HOSPITAL IN AUSTRIA DURING WORLD WAR ONE

ON SOME CAMPS, THE SOLDIERS LIVE IN TENTS THAT CAN BE QUICKLY MOVED AS THE FIGHTING MOVES ON.

SPANISH FLU

At the end of World War One, millions of troops were far from home and living in terrible conditions. There were food and medicine shortages and a killer was coming that nobody was expecting, or ready for.

Four years of war had been very hard on the people of the world. Men living in trenches were living in the wet and mud, packed in close together and unable to stay clean or dry. These are the perfect conditions for a disease to take hold. In the spring of 1918, soldiers in the trenches started complaining of a sore throat, headaches and a loss of appetite. Eventually, people began to develop pneumonia and blood poisoning. Many of these people died. People were moving all around the world as the last months of the war carried on, and when the war was over millions of people slowly started the journey home. This massive movement of people carried this new flu with it…

AMERICAN SOLDIERS IN FRANCE DURING WORLD WAR ONE

THIS IS A DOCTOR'S NOTEBOOK FROM 1918. CAN YOU SEE HOW MANY PATIENTS HERE ARE LISTED AS HAVING INFLUENZA (THE FULL NAME FOR FLU)?

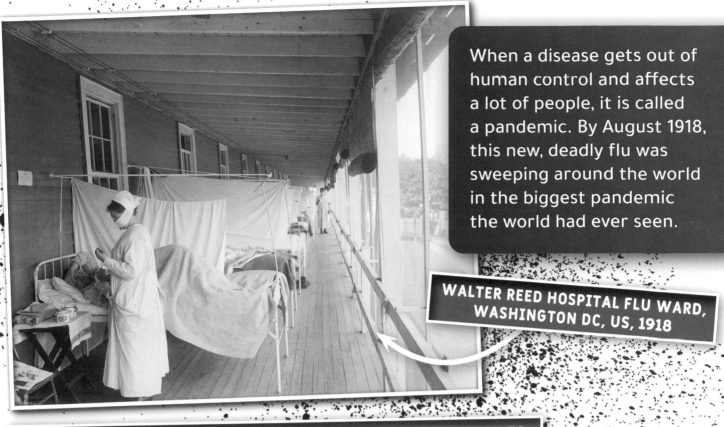

When a disease gets out of human control and affects a lot of people, it is called a pandemic. By August 1918, this new, deadly flu was sweeping around the world in the biggest pandemic the world had ever seen.

WALTER REED HOSPITAL FLU WARD, WASHINGTON DC, US, 1918

MEMBERS OF THE US 39TH REGIMENT IN SEATTLE ON THEIR WAY TO FRANCE IN 1918, WEARING MASKS TO PROTECT THEM AGAINST FLU

Could this new, massive movement of people in the war have caused the pandemic? Possibly. Because people didn't travel much before the war, they didn't come across diseases from other countries at all. This meant their bodies were very weak to these new diseases. As people moved around the world during the war, on a scale never seen before, they took the flu with them. When the whole world came to peace again and people went home, so too did the flu. Spanish flu killed around 50 million people – more than those killed in World War One.

KINDERTRANSPORT

KRISTALLNACHT

Germany was a very terrible place to be <u>Jewish</u> during the lead up to World War Two. A <u>political party</u> called the Nazis were in charge at the time, and they were led by a man called Adolf Hitler. Hitler and the Nazis passed many laws that <u>discriminated</u> against Jewish people.

DURING KRISTALLNACHT, NAZI OFFICIALS ORDERED GERMAN POLICE OFFICERS TO DO NOTHING ABOUT THE VIOLENCE TOWARDS JEWISH PEOPLE, AND FIREFIGHTERS WERE ONLY ALLOWED TO PUT OUT FIRES THAT THREATENED NON-JEWISH BUILDINGS.

On the 7th of November, 1938, a young Polish-Jewish man called Herschel Grynszpan killed a German <u>official</u> in Paris because of Germany's treatment of Jewish people, including his parents. Grynszpan was arrested and the Nazis announced that while they wouldn't punish the Jewish people themselves, they wouldn't stop anyone else from doing so. On the night of the 9th of November, many Jewish homes, <u>synagogues</u> and shops were raided and burnt down, and people were pulled from their homes and beaten. 91 Jewish people were killed, and 30,000 Jewish men were arrested. This night became known as Kristallnacht, which means Crystal Night, or Night of Broken Glass.

JEWISH CHILDREN ALSO ARRIVED IN BRITAIN ON BOATS.

After Kristallnacht, it was too dangerous for Jewish people to stay in Germany. The British <u>government</u> agreed to take in Jewish children under the age of 17 so they could live with <u>foster families</u> until it was safe to go back. This mission became known as Kindertransport. These children had to make the journey to Britain without their parents. They travelled on trains from Germany, Czechoslovakia, Austria and Poland.

10,000 children escaped to Britain on Kindertransport trains. The final train left Berlin on the 1st of September, 1939. This was the day that Hitler invaded Poland and just two days before Britain declared war on Germany.

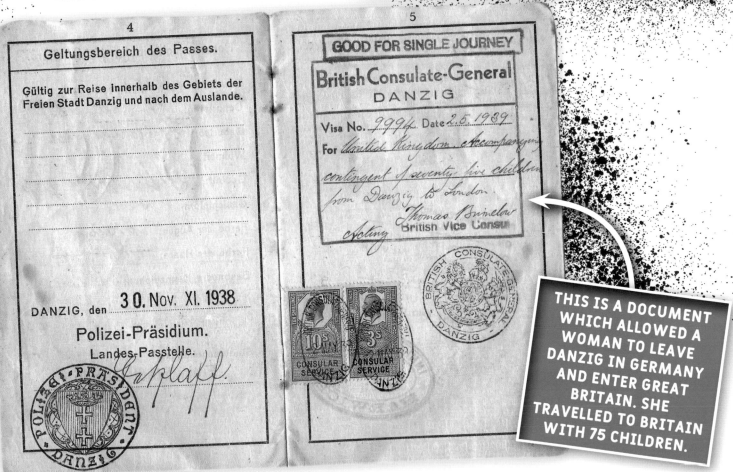

THIS IS A DOCUMENT WHICH ALLOWED A WOMAN TO LEAVE DANZIG IN GERMANY AND ENTER GREAT BRITAIN. SHE TRAVELLED TO BRITAIN WITH 75 CHILDREN.

After the war ended, some of these children were able to return to their families back home. Others who had lost their parents in the war stayed with their foster families in Britain or went to live with family members elsewhere.

EVACUEES

After World War Two had begun, the British government began to worry about enemy air raids. An air raid is when enemy planes drop bombs onto a target below. Most World War Two air raids targeted cities. This made it dangerous to live in cities, so many children were sent to safer parts of the country, mainly in the countryside. Some children were even sent to countries that were not yet at war, such as Canada and the US.

SOME EVACUEE CHILDREN FROM LONDON WENT TO LIVE IN CARMARTHENSHIRE, IN WALES.

Evacuee Fact File

- The evacuations began in September, 1939

- Children who were evacuated were called evacuees

- Families who took children in were called host families

- A home that took in an evacuee child was known as a billet

- Each evacuee was given a gas mask

- Sometimes teachers were evacuated with their classes

- As many as 1.5 million people were evacuated in a few days after World War Two began

EVACUEES HOLDING BOXES WITH GAS MASKS INSIDE

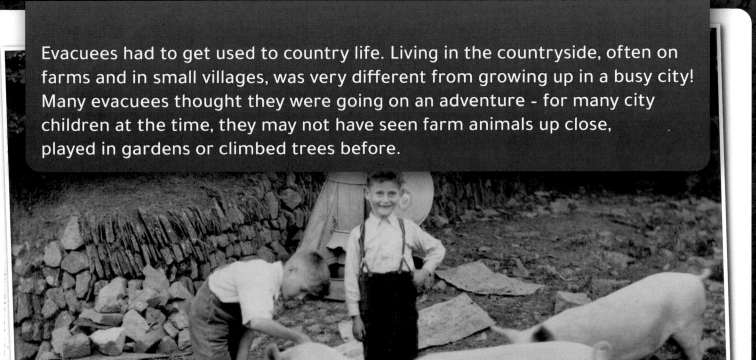

Evacuees had to get used to country life. Living in the countryside, often on farms and in small villages, was very different from growing up in a busy city! Many evacuees thought they were going on an adventure - for many city children at the time, they may not have seen farm animals up close, played in gardens or climbed trees before.

BOYS FROM WHITECHAPEL IN LONDON FEED THE PIGS ON A FARM IN PEMBROKESHIRE

After a few months, not much had happened, and this time came to be known as the Phoney War. Parents, missing their children terribly, called them home and many children were returned. This didn't last for long – within weeks of many children returning to the cities, the bombing started and a period of the war known as the Blitz began. The children were evacuated again – and this time everyone knew exactly why.

THE BLITZ MADE IT EXTREMELY DANGEROUS TO LIVE IN CITIES. IT WAS MUCH SAFER TO LIVE IN THE COUNTRYSIDE WITH A HOST FAMILY. MANY CHILDREN LOVED THEIR HOSTS AND STAYED IN TOUCH WITH THEM AFTER THE WAR.

CONCENTRATION CAMPS

Concentration camps are prisons where people are sent by a government or by the people who invaded the country. The people sent to concentration camps have not committed crimes and are sent without a trial. These people may belong to a group that the government wants to get rid of. This might be during peacetime or as part of a war. People may also be put in camps by an invading army to stop them helping their own army.

THESE WOMEN AND CHILDREN ARE IN A BOER CONCENTRATION CAMP IN SOUTH AFRICA, 1900. THESE CAMPS WERE SET UP BY THE BRITISH DURING THE BOER WAR TO IMPRISON THE BOER PEOPLE.

In 1933, the Nazis in Germany created their first concentration camps, which they said were to hold political prisoners. This would be the beginning of the largest movement of people into camps in history. Anyone who the Nazis wanted to get rid of would be taken to these camps and be locked up, forced to work or even killed.

AUSCHWITZ CONCENTRATION CAMP

During World War Two, millions of people were taken from their homes and towns and sent to these camps. People were moved by train and told that they were going to a work camp or a prison. Men, women and children were all taken. Jewish people were particularly targeted, as were Roma people, disabled people, Slavic people, Black people, gay people and political enemies of the Nazis. Many of these people were killed in the camps or died of starvation, overwork and disease.

THESE JEWISH PEOPLE ARE ARRIVING AT AUSCHWITZ.

It is hard to know exactly how many people were moved to camps during World War Two because the Nazis destroyed any records they kept.

Although historians don't know the exact number, they do know that many millions of people were taken and moved to camps during World War Two.

MAP SHOWING MAJOR CONCENTRATION CAMPS IN NAZI-CONTROLLED AREAS IN WORLD WAR TWO. MILLIONS OF PEOPLE WERE TAKEN FROM ALL OVER THIS AREA TO THESE CAMPS.

✖ = Concentration Camp

FORCED DISPLACEMENT

Forced displacement is when people must leave their homes in order to survive. Forced displacement is common during times of war and conflict, when people's homes and jobs are destroyed, and they are afraid of violence and <u>persecution</u>. By the end of 2018, more than 70 million people were forcibly displaced.

More than two-thirds of all refugees worldwide came from just five countries.

SYRIA

As of 2019, over half of the population of Syria have had to leave their homes because of a civil war that started in 2011. Most Syrians who fled the country arrived in Turkey and Lebanon.

- 22 million people = population before the war
- 5.7 million people = <u>externally displaced</u> people in 2019
- 6.2 million people = <u>internally displaced</u> people in 2019

SOUTH SUDAN

Millions of people have been forced to move from South Sudan to Sudan, Ethiopia, Kenya, Uganda and the Democratic Republic of the Congo because of <u>famine</u>, conflict, violence and civil war.

- 2.3 million people = externally displaced people in 2019
- 1.87 million people = internally displaced people in 2019
- Around 60% of refugees are children

AFGHANISTAN

There have been many wars in Afghanistan, so many people living in the country have had to flee to Iran and Pakistan.

- 1 million people = refugees from Afghanistan in Iran in 2015
- 1.5 million people = refugees from Afghanistan in Pakistan in 2015
- 700,000 people = internally displaced people in 2015

MYANMAR

Hundreds of thousands of Rohingya people in Myanmar face violence and persecution. Since August 2017, around 700,000 Rohingya people have fled Myanmar for Bangladesh.

- Around 1 million people = population of Rohingya people in Myanmar at the start of 2017
- 484,000 people = number of Rohingya people in Myanmar in October 2017, including internally displaced people
- 947,000 people = number of Rohingya people in Bangladesh in October 2017

SOMALIA

Terrorist groups are in charge of large parts of Somalia, and there are many ongoing conflicts that have lasted for many years. A lot of the country is unsafe to live in, so many people have been forced to move away.

- Over 870,000 people = externally displaced people in 2018
- 2.1 million people = internally displaced people in 2018

HOMECOMING

After a war has ended, there are still a lot of people to move around. Troops on the <u>front line</u> must return to their homes. In a big conflict like a world war, this can mean having to organise the transport of millions of people from hundreds of countries all back to the right place. The process of returning all the troops, camps and equipment is called demobilisation, or demobbing.

BRITISH SERVICEMEN ON THEIR WAY HOME AFTER WORLD WAR TWO

DEMOBBED SERVICEMEN AFTER WORLD WAR TWO WERE GIVEN A NEW SUIT TO HELP THEM RETURN TO ORDINARY LIFE AFTER THE WAR. IT WAS KNOWN AS A DEMOB SUIT.

PUSH BAR

After World War One and World War Two, everyone wanted to get home as soon as possible. Unfortunately, this couldn't be done. Millions of people needed to be officially returned to their countries and given the proper papers, medical care, money and clothing - all of which they needed in order to start their lives as ordinary people again.

After both world wars, it took years to return all the people to their home countries. There was lots of paperwork before soldiers could be released from service. Men who had the most important jobs back home were released first, and then everyone else depending on their age, how long they had served and how many times they had been wounded in battle.

A CERTIFICATE OF DEMOBILISATION

THIS BRITISH SOLDIER IS AT NO. 1 BRITISH TRANSIT CAMP, NEE SOON, SINGAPORE, WAITING TO BE SENT HOME.

THESE BRITISH SOLDIERS ARE HEADING BACK HOME FROM SINGAPORE.

AMERICAN TROOPS ON THEIR WAY HOME FROM ENGLAND

A LAND DOWN UNDER

Straight after the end of World War Two, the Australian government realised that its population levels were very low. They needed more people to be able to defend and develop the country. Prime Minister Ben Chifley announced the creation of the Federal Department of Immigration. They would solve their population problem by simply moving new people in! Their slogan was 'Populate or Perish!' and they presented Australia as a land of new opportunity, far away from Europe. They wanted to welcome families and young, working-age people with open arms.

THESE MIGRANTS ARE ARRIVING IN AUSTRALIA ON A SHIP.

THESE MIGRANTS FROM CZECHOSLOVAKIA ARE HEADING FOR MELBOURNE, AUSTRALIA.

BETWEEN 1945 AND 1965, MORE THAN 2 MILLION MIGRANTS ARRIVED IN AUSTRALIA. THIS MEANT THERE WERE LOTS OF YOUNGER PEOPLE WHO WERE READY TO WORK.

IMMIGRANTS WHO CAME INTO THE COUNTRY WERE KNOWN AS NEW AUSTRALIANS.

Migrant = someone who moves from one country to another by choice

Economic migrant = someone who leaves their own country to find better work in another country

Immigrant = someone who moves into another country

Emigrant = someone who moves out of their own country

Australia
land of tomorrow

THIS POSTER WAS MADE BY THE AUSTRALIAN GOVERNMENT AND WAS DISPLAYED BETWEEN 1949 AND 1951 IN RECEPTION CENTRES FOR MIGRANTS ARRIVING IN AUSTRALIA. WHY DO YOU THINK IT IS SO COLOURFUL AND JOYFUL?

A POST-WAR WORLD

Wars can cause massive movements of people but also stop any movement as well. Countries at war may close their borders and stop people from moving around and leaving. Sometimes no one can enter or leave a country at war.

Towards the end of World War Two, it looked like the Allies were going to defeat Germany and win the war. The Allies decided that Germany would be split into four zones. The Soviet Union, Britain, France and the US would each control a zone. Britain, France and the US took control of areas in the west, and the Soviet Union took control of the east. Berlin, the capital of Germany, was to be inside the Soviet zone, but this too would be split into four zones.

BERLIN

GERMANY

THE ALLIES WERE GREAT BRITAIN, FRANCE, THE SOVIET UNION AND THE US. THEY FOUGHT TOGETHER IN WORLD WAR TWO AGAINST GERMANY, ITALY AND JAPAN.

GREAT BRITAIN, THE US AND THE SOVIET UNION DISCUSSED THE BREAKING UP OF GERMANY AT SOMETHING CALLED THE YALTA CONFERENCE. LEADERS OF THE THREE COUNTRIES – PRIME MINISTER WINSTON CHURCHILL, PRESIDENT FRANKLIN ROOSEVELT AND SOVIET LEADER JOSEPH STALIN – WERE THERE.

As soon as it was decided what would happen to Germany, it was time to decide what would happen to the millions of German people spread across Europe. The Allies decided that German people in Poland, Czechoslovakia, Hungary and elsewhere in eastern Europe needed to be sent back to Germany. Some of these people had only just arrived in those countries, but others had been born there and had always thought of it as being their home. This movement of people was the largest population movement in European history.

MANY GERMAN REFUGEES, SOMETIMES CALLED EXPELLEES, STAYED IN CAMPS LIKE THIS ONE.

SOME EXPELLEES LIVED IN SETTLEMENTS, SUCH AS THIS ONE IN ESPELKAMP, GERMANY.

THE BERLIN WALL

TWO GERMANIES

By 1949, Germany had been split into two countries: the Federal Republic of Germany (FDR), or West Germany, and the German Democratic Republic (GDR), or East Germany. West Germany was made up of the British, US and French zones and East Germany was made up of the Soviet zone. The two countries were run very differently – in West Germany, people were free to move around, listen to different kinds of music and express their opinions on things. In East Germany, there were strict rules on how people should behave.

EAST GERMANY

BERLIN

WEST GERMANY

BORDER BETWEEN EAST BERLIN AND WEST BERLIN

The four zones of Berlin were also grouped to create West Berlin and East Berlin. While the border between West Germany and East Germany was closed to prevent people leaving East Germany, the border between West Berlin and East Berlin was open. Many people used the border in Berlin to escape from the east to the west.

In 1961, Nikita Khrushchev, the leader of the Soviet Union at the time, announced that the border between East and West Berlin was closed and no more people could cross. He ordered a wall to be built to stop people crossing from East Berlin into West Berlin. The wall started off as <u>barbed wire</u> and fencing, and was put up overnight on the 13th of August, 1961. Over time, it became a long line of strong walls, fences and watchtowers. The wall was 155 kilometres long and four metres tall. <u>Checkpoints</u> were set up to stop people, and the most famous of all was known as Checkpoint Charlie.

CHECKPOINT CHARLIE IN DECEMBER 1961...

... AND YEARS LATER, STILL THERE IN 1985.

THE FALL OF THE BERLIN WALL

Around 5,000 people tried to escape to West Berlin over the Berlin Wall, but it was very dangerous – more than 100 people were killed for doing so. In the 1980s, people began to protest how the Soviet Union controlled lots of countries, including East Germany and East Berlin. People wanted the freedom to live their lives how they wanted to live them, and to move wherever they wanted to.

In 1987, American president Ronald Reagan made a famous speech at the Brandenburg Gate in West Berlin. President Reagan challenged the head of the Soviet Union, Mikhail Gorbachev, to allow more freedom in East Germany and East Berlin.

" WE WELCOME CHANGE AND OPENNESS, FOR WE BELIEVE THAT FREEDOM AND SECURITY GO TOGETHER [...] GENERAL SECRETARY GORBACHEV, IF YOU SEEK PEACE [...] COME HERE TO THIS GATE. MR GORBACHEV, OPEN THIS GATE [...] MR GORBACHEV, TEAR DOWN THIS WALL! "

PRESIDENT REAGAN IN FRONT OF THE BRANDENBURG GATE, WEST BERLIN, 1987

After speeches from both President Ronald Reagan and President John F Kennedy, and many protests from Germans and people from around the world, on the 9th of November, 1989, the leader of East Germany announced that the border between the two countries would be opened. Finally, after 21 years, the movement of people in Germany was free and open once again.

PRESIDENT JOHN F KENNEDY VISITING THE BERLIN WALL IN 1963

Thousands of East Germans rushed to the wall. The guards couldn't hold everyone back, so they had to step back and watch as they all crossed the wall into West Berlin.

For weeks after, people slowly began destroying the wall with hammers, ropes, and anything else they could find. In 1990, the government finally destroyed the wall. They left many parts of it standing so people can see it still today.

ON THE 3RD OF OCTOBER, 1990, EAST AND WEST GERMANY WERE REUNITED AND BECAME ONE COUNTRY AGAIN.

MANY GERMANS CELEBRATED THE FALL OF THE BERLIN WALL BY CLIMBING TO THE TOP.

WHILE THE WALL WAS STANDING, HUNDREDS OF EAST GERMANS MANAGED TO ESCAPE BY FLEEING TO COUNTRIES THAT WERE CLOSE TO GERMANY, SUCH AS HUNGARY AND CZECHOSLOVAKIA.

ACTIVITY

STORY OF AN EVACUEE

Imagine you are an evacuee in World War Two. You have been sent to the countryside because it is safer than the city. Use what you have learnt on pages 14 and 15 to write a story about what happens to you. How do you get there? Who takes care of you? What is their house like? Are you scared or excited? You can draw pictures for your story.

THINGS TO THINK ABOUT

It is important that everyone around the world helps those who are running away from war. Other countries must make sure that there is a safe place for these people to go. In a group, try to come up with some ideas to help people who lost their home because of war. What will they need? How could you make them feel at home in a new place?

GLOSSARY

allied part of or to do with the Allies, a group of countries including France, Great Britain, the Soviet Union and the US who fought in World War Two

barbed wire spiky metal wire that is dangerous to touch

blockades things that are put in place to stop people or goods from going in or out of a place

checkpoints barriers with people guarding them, who check who is passing through

compromise when different sides of an argument agree on something by giving up things or making sacrifices

deployed moved troops

discriminated treated a person unfairly based on illogical reasons, such as gender, sex, age, where they are from or what they look like

empires groups of countries or states that are owned by one ruler or country

externally displaced when people are forced to leave their homes and go into another country

famine when large numbers of people do not have enough food

foster families families that bring up a child that isn't related to them

front line the place in a war which is closest to the enemy

gas mask a mask that protects the wearer from dangerous gases

government the group of people with the power to run a country and decide its laws

infrastructure the basic services, such as a power supply and roads, that a community needs in order to function

internally displaced when people are forced to leave their homes and stay somewhere else, still in the same country

Jewish to do with the religion of Judaism

officers (in an army) high-ranking or important soldiers

official (in politics) someone with an important job in an organisation, such as the government

persecution cruel or unfair treatment based on religion, political beliefs, where a person is from or what they look like

pneumonia a serious, sometimes fatal, lung infection

political party a group of people who have the same political ideas, who want to be part of the government

political prisoners people who are put in prison for their political beliefs

politics ideas or activities to do with how a country should be run

protest an action that shows disagreement with something

Roma people a group of people who live all over the world, but mostly in Europe, many of whom speak a Romany language

Slavic people a group of people who speak a group of languages called Slavonic, who often come from Eastern Europe or Asian Russia

spies people who secretly get information from the enemy

synagogues Jewish religious buildings

terrorist to do with people who do violent things to make people listen or follow their political ideas

trial an event where specially chosen people try to fairly decide if criminals are guilty or not

INDEX